Straight Talk to

MEN

and Their Wives

Other books by Dr. James C. Dobson

Dare to Discipline
The Mentally Retarded Child and His Family
    (co-edited with Dr. Richard Koch)
Hide or Seek
What Wives Wish Their Husbands Knew about Women
The Strong-Willed Child
Preparing for Adolescence

For complete list of other materials for the family see page 221.

Dr. James C. Dobson

Straight Talk to
MEN
and Their Wives

First Key-Word Printing

Scripture quotations marked NIV from The Holy Bible, New International
Version, copyright © 1978 by New York International Bible Society.
Scripture quotation marked PHILLIPS from The New Testament in Modern
English, copyright 1958, 1959, 1960 by J. B. Phillips; used by permission of the
Macmillan Company. Scripture quotations marked TLB from The Living Bible,
Paraphrased (Wheaton: Tyndale House Publishers, 1971) and used by permis-
sion. Scripture quotations marked RSV from the Revised Standard Version of
the Bible, copyrighted 1946, 1952, © 1971, 1973 by the Division of Christian
Education of the National Council of the Churches of Christ in the U.S.A.,
and used by permission.

ISBN 0-8499-4165-2
Library of Congress catalog card number: 80-51595
Printed in the United States of America

Illustrations by Dennis Bellile

This book is affectionately dedicated to the memory of my father, James Dobson, Sr., for reasons which will be understood as these pages are read.